The FIRST BOOK of

ANCIENT
MESOPOTAMIA
and
PERSIA

Stone animal from the ruins of Persepolis.

The FIRST BOOK OF

ANCIENT

MESOPOTAMIA

and

PERSIA

by Charles Alexander Robinson, Jr.

ILLUSTRATED WITH MAPS AND PHOTOGRAPHS

FRANKLIN WATTS, INC.

575 Lexington Avenue • New York 22

TO MY DAUGHTERS-IN-LAW

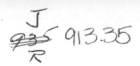
Contents

Buried under the drifting sands.

The Ancient Near East

ALONG the eastern coast of the Mediterranean Sea and stretching eastward into Asia lies a part of the world that gave birth to some of the most important civilizations on our planet. This part of the world is known as the ancient Near East. As land areas go, it is a large part of the world indeed, for it includes Egypt, Palestine, Syria, neighboring Asia Minor, and the land of Mesopotamia, now called Iraq.

Civilization began so long ago that we shall probably never know where it really started. It may have been in Mesopotamia, or in Egypt in the valley of the River Nile, or even in far-off India in the valley of the Indus River, or somewhere else. It may even have begun in several places at the same time. The Sumerians, who were among the earliest people to live in Mesopotamia, said that civilization began in Paradise, the "Garden of the Gods," which they placed beside the Persian Gulf, into which the rivers of Mesopotamia flow. Here, they said, the gods, in their infinite love for men, kindly allowed civilization to commence.

Wherever it began, we know that a highly developed civilization was flourishing in Mesopotamia as long ago as 3000 B.C. For centuries it lay buried under the drifting sands of a desert waste. Then, during the twentieth century, archeologists began to uncover the great mounds of earth that dot the plain in that part of the world. Little by little they uncovered the houses, tombs, sculptures, writings, and even the bodies of an ancient people who not only made a remarkable civilization for themselves, but also helped create our own European civilization.

1

And so we begin our story of civilization with the Sumerians and with the Babylonians, who followed along in history right after them. Then we shall see how a people to the north, known as the Assyrians, began to create a great empire in the land, until the Persians united the entire Near East in a "world state," as men of those days described it.

All these civilizations — Sumerian, Babylonian, Assyrian, and Persian — influenced one another. Later, they influenced Greece and Rome, whose civilizations spread through Europe to the British Isles and finally to America.

Land of the Two Rivers

MESOPOTAMIA means "between the rivers" — that is, the land between the rivers Tigris and Euphrates, which rise in the mountains of Armenia, far to the north. Travel and communication were easy in Mesopotamia, particularly in the lower or southern part of the region, where the country is very flat. The early inhabitants traveled back and forth along the two rivers for a distance of a thousand miles.

For short trips, three or four men might use a raft made of animal skins and reeds. As many as ninety people, bound for places at a distance, might embark as passengers on flat-bottomed boats forty-five feet in length. Sails were used to propel the boats, except along narrow canals or in swamps, where the crews used poles to push their craft along. Toiling along the river banks, men with strong ropes towed barges loaded with food and other necessities.

Over the flat land between the rivers, people traveled afoot or on donkeyback. Camels were scarce, and horses were not known in Mesopotamia until 2000 B.C., when they were brought in by invaders.

In time, traders followed the rivers south into the Persian Gulf and so were able to get down to the Indian Ocean, which is part of the Pacific Ocean. But in the beginning people did not travel far, and they had little idea of what the world was like beyond the two rivers. We know this to be so because they left behind them a clay map of the "world." It shows the sea running from the Persian Gulf to the Caucasus Mountains and back again. All the inhabitants of the world, they believed, lived on the land surrounded by this sea.

But as the Mesopotamians traveled up and down their rivers, whether on errands of peace or war, their world was widening little by little. The travelers met new peoples and discovered new ways of life. Traders exchanged not only goods but also ideas. Men's minds were stimulated to think new thoughts and to invent things.

New experiences, new ideas — these are the things that make civilizations grow. And so it was that the ease of travel and communication played an important part in the development of civilization in the ancient Near East.

Government Comes into Being

AN EVEN more important part was played by climate. Southern Mesopotamia is very hot, and the condensation of water from the two rivers keeps the air moist. This is the ideal climate for the date palm. Fruit is always the special diet of people in hot countries, and dates are among the most valuable of fruits because they can be prepared in so many different ways — as a kind of bread, as a drink resembling wine, and as a sweet somewhat like honey. But date palms must have water, and there is little rain in southern Mesopotamia. If the early Sumerians wanted plenty of dates to eat, they had to water the palm trees. This meant that they had to dig irrigation canals, and that was too big a job for a single man. The whole community had to work at it together.

Still another factor caused the people to work together in this land between the rivers, and that was the rivers themselves. Every spring, when the snows melt in the mountains, the Tigris and the Euphrates overflow their banks. In doing so, they spread over the land the rich soil, or "silt," they have carried along in their floods. The Sumerians were well on their way to civilizing themselves when they learned to plant crops in this rich new earth.

The floods, however, were a mixed blessing. If they were not controlled, they would drown the people and ruin the villages. So the villagers had to learn how to dig ditches to channel the water to their fields and gardens. And since the dry season lasted a long time, they had to find ways to store the excess floodwater for future use. Again the people had to work together on projects that were too big for one man to handle alone.

Now we shall see how working together led to government — the establishment of law and order — without which no civilization can exist.

When people undertake a big community project, such as flood control, there must be a leader to plan and direct the work. Eventually the leaders in Mesopotamia became kings. They surrounded themselves with officials to help them collect taxes, administer justice, promote trade, organize the army, and so on. When this happened, government was born.

It was easy to bring southern Mesopotamia under one government, even in the early days. A king and his army could march now here, now there over the flat land between the rivers. But it was just as easy for a foreign invader to march in with his army. Therefore, as time went on, governments occasionally changed.

4

Clay plaque, 3300 B.C., showing a Sumerian king receiving tribute.

An Expanding World

THE VILLAGES in the land of the two rivers grew into cities where lived both rich and poor, the priests, the government officials, and artisans such as carpenters and metal workers. Gone was the simple community of farmers and traders that had been ruled by the leader. Gone, too, was the tiny world surrounded by the sea. The travelers were venturing far from home.

Directly to the west of southern Mesopotamia is the huge

Arabian Desert. Men dreaded to cross it when they began to travel and trade. They went north with the Tigris and the Euphrates, where they would find plenty of food and water. After they had traveled north for a few hundred miles, they discovered that the cultivated land curved westward. Finally they found that if they followed this rich land curving to the west, this so-called "Fertile Crescent," they would come to the Mediterranean Sea. Here were Syria and Palestine and, to the south, Egypt.

Most of the men of Mesopotamia and the eastern Mediterranean coast, though not all of them, belonged to the branch of the human race known as "Semites." Among them were Arabs, Hebrews, Syrians, Babylonians, and Assyrians. The men of southern Mesopotamia exchanged goods with those of the Mediterranean coast, and before long they exchanged ideas and customs, too. Civilization had begun not only to grow but to expand beyond the narrow confines of the two rivers.

The Remarkable Sumerians

IN THE Old Testament of the Bible it is written: "And Terah took Abraham . . . and Sarah his daughter-in-law, his son Abraham's wife; and they went forth with them from Ur of the Chaldees."

Sumer, as the region in southern Mesopotamia was called, was a land of cities, and the chief city from 3000 to 2000 B.C. was Ur. It was in Ur, home of the patriarch Abraham, that scientists of the twentieth century were to unearth many of the treasures that help tell the story of Sumerian civilization.

A distinguished American archeologist, Samuel Noah Kramer, has shown that everything the Sumerians did was done for the first time, at least in this part of the world. Since these people knew nothing about the rest of the world, we might say that they spent their time inventing first one important thing and then another.

For example, they realized that if they were ever to be anything but wandering nomads, living on wild fruit and the like, they must sow the land with seed and stay around long enough to harvest the crop. We have seen how they dug reservoirs, canals, and ditches to water their fields. As mud collected in this irrigation system, they cleaned it out. They built dikes to protect their villages against the floods. And we know that these community projects led not only to government, but also to settled life in cities.

How the Sumerians Built Their Houses

The first houses of the Sumerians were nothing more than simple huts. A man would cut down some reeds in the swamp and make bundles of them. Then he would fix one of the bundles in the earth and bend it over until it made an arch, with the other end also fixed in the earth. When he had arranged a number of these arches next to each other, he would have a kind of tunnel along whose sides he would tie other bundles of reeds in horizontal rows to serve as walls. On top, he would throw mats of reeds to make a roof.

It was not long before the Sumerians learned that they could make an excellent building material by scooping together some earth from the Mesopotamian plain, pouring water on it, cutting it into bricks, and letting the bricks dry in the sun and the wind. It was possible to build a house very quickly with these sun-dried mud bricks, and the house would last a long time in the dry climate. When, eventually, the occasional rains wore the bricks down and melted them back into earth, a man could level off the remains of his house and build another on top of them.

Because of the ever-present danger of floods, the Sumerians built their large buildings, such as palaces and temples, on artificial mounds of earth. Most of these buildings, like the houses, were

7

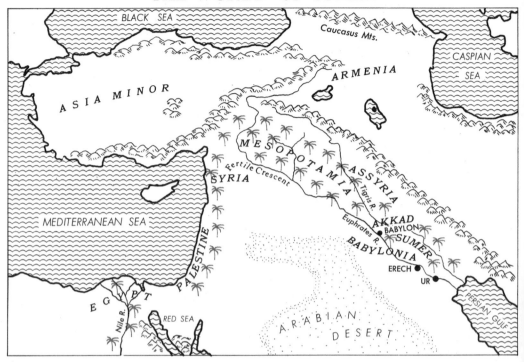

made of mud bricks, because Mesopotamia lacked suitable stone and timber. A few were made of bricks baked in an oven. In time, all of these buildings collapsed, burying in their ruins the material remains of life.

It was probably an inconvenience for the Sumerians to keep building and rebuilding as they did, but it was a great good fortune for us. When the walls of a mud brick building collapsed, they buried under them countless treasures for archeologists to discover in later centuries. We can imagine how a great mound of earth would come into existence as one building after another rose upon the ruins of the last. It is these mounds that dot the entire Mesopotamian plain, inviting archeologists to dig them. Some of the mounds have already been excavated, but much work remains to be done. In fact, archeology, which is a branch of history, cries aloud for more students, both men and women.

Interior of a Sumerian house, 3000 B.C.

How They Farmed the Land

Just as the Sumerians improved their homes — from reed huts to brick houses — so too did they develop their agriculture. In the beginning they plowed the ground with stone hoes and cut their grain with clay sickles. Then they learned how to use metals, and broke the ground with metal plows. These plows had funnel-shaped containers on them which the farmers filled with seed. As the oxen pulled the plows, the seed filtered down through the funnels into the earth. It was a quick and easy way of doing the planting.

Before anyone else in history, Sumerian farmers had handbooks that told them exactly what to do to insure a successful crop. First, a man must irrigate and weed his field and fence it in against animals. (Things would go better if he had already planted shade trees to protect his garden from the wind and sun.) Then he must plow and plant and water the ground. This done, he should pray for a good crop and do what he could to frighten away the birds.

When the grain ripened, the farmer would cut it with a copper sickle, for the days of the old clay sickle had passed long ago. He would thresh the grain by pulling a heavy stone across the stalks, and winnow it by throwing it into the air to separate the chaff from the good grain.

Wheat and barley were the most important grains grown by the Sumerians. Fruits included the ever-popular dates, and also grapes, figs, melons, and apples. The favorite vegetable was eggplant, which more or less took the place of our potato. But the Sumerians also grew onions, radishes, beans, and lettuce.

Around a man's farm roamed dogs and chickens, pigs, sheep, goats, cattle, oxen, and buffaloes. Sprightly gazelles ran across the plains, and lions lurked in the reeds along with jackals, foxes,

Door of a Sumerian temple. The blocks of stone used for flooring were brought from other lands.

panthers, and wild boars. The Sumerians used spears to hunt these animals. They caught fish in nets and traps, and brought down birds with clay slingshots or with arrows.

Government and Law

The Sumerians were the first people in history to develop a simple form of self-rule, or democracy. It is true that the kings of the various cities, in consultation with the chief priests and councils of old men, decided most things. But the most important question of all — whether to make peace or war — was left to assemblies of free adult men.

Of first importance in a civilized society is a written code, or collection, of laws. When laws are not written down, unjust officials can claim that the laws are known only to themselves, and they can twist them as they choose. The Sumerians were the first people in history to write down the laws they passed. From this written code of laws, we know that the people of Sumer were humane and sought justice for everybody. For example, Sumerian laws said that a widow or an orphan could not be taxed; they protected ordinary people from the rich and powerful; and they tried to give all people freedom and security.

Religion and Learning

The Sumerians realized that the universe is governed by forces stronger than ourselves. These forces they called gods. The most powerful of all was Anu, who represented authority. Next came Inanna, goddess of love and war. Later on, the Babylonians worshiped Inanna under the name of Ishtar.

The Sumerians believed that it was their duty to provide the gods with food, drink, and shelter. Every city had a temple, or at least a terrace, where the various gods could live, and where the people could go to worship and be near them. Priests conducted the religious services, which included the singing of hymns to the accompaniment of drums, flutes, and lyres. The people believed that they were responsible for their own suffering, and they prayed to the gods to help them relieve or prevent it.

Before any other people in history, the Sumerians had schools. Only rich boys were lucky enough to attend, however. These boys learned grammar, mathematics, literature, and how to study the stars and planets. They were taught by scribes — official or public writers who acted as clerks — and most students hoped to become scribes themselves, or else government officials.

Archeologists tell us that some people in Sumer studied medicine. We do not know what diseases doctors treated, or whether their cures worked. We do know, however, that the Sumerians did not depend on the gods or on magic to heal them, as primitive people do. To make a salve to put on wounds, doctors ground dried pears, figs, and dates into a powder and poured olive oil over it. For certain illnesses, they prescribed unappetizing powders dissolved in milk and beer to kill the taste. They used salt as an anti-

OF ART, PURCHASE, 1886.

THE METROPOLITAN MUSEUM

Over 4000 years ago a schoolboy in Sumeria used this clay tablet to practise his writing lesson.

septic (a very sensible custom), and saltpeter (potassium nitrate) as an astringent. Surgeons knew how to attend to very simple things such as broken bones. Dentists could extract teeth.

Before they were conquered by the Babylonians, the Sumerians had invented a calendar and a system of weights and measures, which the Babylonians adopted.

All in all, the Sumerian civilization was so beautiful and worthwhile, and so much a part of the region where it had developed, that it influenced all future civilizations, especially the Babylonian one that followed it.

The Clay Tablets

The most important of all Sumerian inventions was writing. At first, it consisted simply of pictures. Then these remarkable people invented signs to represent words and the syllables of words. These they impressed by means of triangular, or wedge-shaped, reeds on

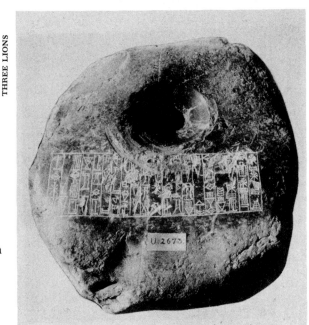

THREE LIONS

Clay tablet covered with cuneiform writing.

clay tablets while the tablets were still moist and soft. Because the Latin word for wedge is *cuneus,* scholars in later centuries called this kind of writing *cuneiform.* Among the buried treasures of Sumer, archeologists have found whole libraries consisting of clay tablets covered with this cuneiform writing. They have even found the catalog of a Sumerian library listing over sixty works of literature.

Archeology tells us a great deal about early Mesopotamia, but our ability to read what was written with the strange cuneiform signs on the clay tablets tells us even more. How scholars learned to decipher the signs is a fascinating story in itself.

There were a number of different languages spoken in Mesopotamia, for various proud peoples flourished there during a period of 3,000 years. About 500 B.C., a Persian king, Darius I, carved a long inscription on a cliff at Behistun, above the road that runs from Babylon to Ecbatana in modern Persia. Darius' inscription was a boastful tribute to himself and the glories of his reign, and since he wanted everybody to be able to read it, he carved it in several different languages, including Persian and Babylonian. Not many people could get near enough to it to read it, however, for the cliff is sharp and steep and is 155 feet high.

Until the middle of the nineteenth century, the inscription on the cliff at Behistun remained a mystery to the modern world. Then two great scholars — one a German named George Grotefend, the other an Englishman named Sir Henry Rawlinson — figured out what a few of the cuneiform signs meant. Suddenly they realized that the ancient Persian language, in which part of the inscription was written, was very much like the language of the *Avesta,* a collection of sacred hymns and prayers written in ancient Persian and read by people in Persia and India today. By learning

The cliff at Behistun, on which Darius
inscribed his victories in three languages.

to read ancient Persian and matching the Persian words with words written in the other languages, Grotefend and Rawlinson were able to translate all the other languages carved on the cliff. With the key supplied by these two men, scholars were able to read the poems and literature written in cuneiform on the clay tablets of the Sumerians.

Digging for the Past

IN ORDER to carry on an excavation, an archeologist (or the university or museum to which he is attached) has first to find financial backing. Then, after he has secured the permission of the particular country in which he wants to dig, he gathers together his staff of archeological assistants, architects, artists, photographers, and so on. Various local foremen and laborers complete the expedition. The chief tools used in digging are picks and shovels.

The archeologist has certain things he goes by in choosing his site. There may be a story, passed down from generation to generation over the centuries, that a city once stood on a certain spot. Better still, there may be a mound of earth or part of a building standing above ground. One thing is a certain clue to the archeologist in search of ancient cities: wherever people lived in ancient times, there will be broken pieces of pottery, known as sherds, scattered about on the ground. These are the remains of clay dishes, cups, and pitchers used by people centuries ago. Since they were usually baked in ovens, they are practically indestructible.

Excavating is a slow and careful business. Everything that is found on the site is recorded. The vases, sculptures, and other small discoveries are safely stored away. Every building or part of a building is drawn and photographed. The diggers go deeper and deeper into the earth until they reach hardpan, or undisturbed

17

soil, known to archeologists as "stereo." Digging stops at this point because no one ever lived at a lower level and so nothing will be found.

After all the findings of the diggers have been carefully studied, the results are published in a book so that people everywhere may share the archeologists' discoveries and learn from them.

From the Graves of Ancient Kings

Shortly after World War I, a famous English archeologist named Sir Leonard Woolley was sent by the British Museum and the University of Pennsylvania to excavate the royal cemetery of Ur in the ancient land of the Sumerians. Among the astonishing treasures the archeologist found were gold helmets and cups; lyres made of gold and silver, white shell, red limestone, and lapis lazuli (an azure-blue stone containing sulphur); shell ornaments; and gold and silver jewelry. These treasures told Woolley a great deal not only about the religion and artistic taste of the Sumerians, but also about the extent of their travels and trade. For example, the lapis lazuli must have come from northwestern India, for there is none in Mesopotamia. The nickel used in making the bronze weapons that were found in the cemetery must, for the same reason, have come from east of the Persian Gulf. It was clear that the Sumerians had traveled to these areas to trade with the people there.

Ur's royal cemetery consisted of underground tombs that look like large rooms built of bricks. In ancient times, there were pits in front of them. In one of these pits, Woolley found the skeletons of sixty-four women. It is a good guess that when a king or queen died, the Sumerians killed members of their court, who then supposedly accompanied the soul of their ruler to the lower world.

Today the treasures found in the royal cemetery of Ur — the

golden vessels, the musical instruments that long ago were laid away with the dead to comfort them in the dark and gloomy underworld — are exhibited in the British Museum of London, the University Museum of Philadelphia, and the Baghdad Museum in Iraq.

The Great Flood
> "And the waters prevailed . . . upon the earth."
> — *The Book of Genesis*

Hoping to find more treasure, Woolley extended his digging below the tombs. He found nothing but dirt and sand. To the ordinary person, this might have been a great disappointment, but to Woolley it opened up an exciting possibility. Dirt and sand were just what one might have expected to find where there had once been a great flood. This particular flood might have been caused by overwhelming waters from the Persian Gulf.

Like most people from the Western World, Woolley knew the Biblical story of the flood that covered the world. He also knew that the ancient Hebrews, whose history is to be found in the Old Testament of the Bible, traced their ancestry back to the patriarch Abraham. It was Abraham who, at God's bidding, left Ur for Palestine not long after 1800 B.C. Woolley asked himself whether Abraham and his fellow Semites might have known of a great flood at Ur, one big and devastating enough to have made people believe it covered the whole earth.

Woolley dug a pit sixty feet down through the dirt and sand. At the bottom of it, he found a settlement that had once been buried by a flood. Nobody knows, of course, whether or not this flood inspired the Biblical story, but it is an interesting fact that archeological discoveries in Mesopotamia prove more and more that the Old Testament is historically true.

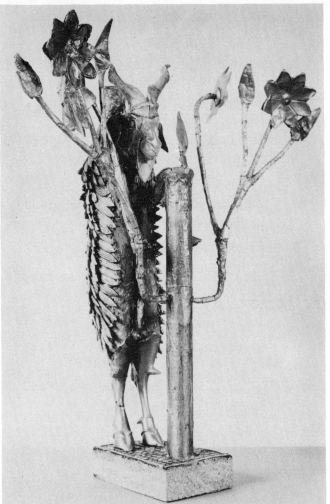

"Ram in the Thicket." The animal's face and legs are of gold, the belly is of silver, and the beard, horns, and pupils of the eyes are of lapis lazuli. The fleece is made of white shell.

Tiny doe made of gold.

Statuette of a temple worshipper.

A king's golden helmet.

TREASURES
FROM
THE CITY OF UR

Magnificent bull's head of gold and lapis lazuli.

Kitchen of a priest. The stone on which the native is sitting was probably used to grind grain into meal for bread.

The Fall of Sumer

We still do not know where the Sumerians came from. We do not even know whether they were Semites, but it is certain that their language was not Semitic. We do know, however, that the land of Akkad, just to the north of the Sumerians, was Semitic.

The most powerful king of Akkad was Sargon. The story of how he became king is an interesting example of how the legends of one country may become, in time, the legends of another.

Sargon's mother, the Akkadians said, was of very humble origin. Nobody knew who his father was. Sargon was born in a secret place, and soon afterward his mother put him in a basket and set him adrift on the Euphrates River. He was rescued by a simple irrigator and brought up to be a gardener. But the great Semitic goddess, Ishtar, loved him and made him king. He ruled for forty-five years.

22

The Romans, whose culture was influenced by the culture of Mesopotamia, had a similar explanation for the founding of their city. Twin boys, Romulus and Remus, were set adrift on the Tiber River, cast ashore, and nursed by a she-wolf. Then one of them, Romulus, founded Rome.

The people of Sumer and Akkad were often at war with each other. Then, about 2000 B.C., they were both overwhelmed by powerful invaders. These were the Semitic Amorites, who made Babylon, on the Euphrates, their capital. Ever afterward the land around them, including Sumer and Akkad, was called Babylonia. The Babylonians quickly absorbed Sumerian culture and brought Mesopotamia to a tremendous peak of civilization as a result.

The Babylonians

Gate of the Gods

The capital of Babylonia, and the center of its great civilization, was Babylon. The narrow streets of this luxurious city were lined with private houses. Stout cedar beams supported the flat roofs where families often slept on warm nights. Rich men built their walls of baked bricks but, since fuel was scarce, the poor used unbaked mud bricks, as in earlier times. Rich and poor alike often covered their outside walls with stucco.

In general, a Babylonian house looked plain and uninteresting from outside, for it had no windows opening on the street. But the interior of the house, even if it only belonged to a moderately prosperous Babylonian, was comfortably furnished with beautiful tables, chairs, beds, and other furniture. Floors were made of baked brick. On the second floor were the bedrooms. Downstairs were the living and dining rooms. Food was cooked in a kitchen in

The tumbled ruins of Babylon.

bronze pots and pans shaped much like our own, and water was drawn from a private well. Every house had a chapel, where the gods were worshiped, and members of the family were buried.

One of the most attractive features of a Babylonian house was the interior court, open to the sky, where people could walk and talk. This court provided the house with air and light during the day. At night, light was furnished by lamps in which olive oil was burned.

Babylon was called the "Gate of the Gods," and the traveler approaching the city from the plain must easily have understood the reason why. Palaces and temples towered into the sky. Because of the ever-present danger of floods, these buildings were built on

24

earthen mounds, or platforms, that might cover several acres.

Babylonian temples were shaped like the pyramids of Egypt, and might rise seventy feet from their mounds in a series of steps, or terraces, known as "ziggurats." Walls were of baked bricks with colorful facings of enamel.

These buildings were very impressive, for the skillful architects knew how to span an opening and support weight from above by the use of curved arches. Ceilings and roofs were formed by arched vaults, and the whole might be held up by columns. These architectural features, like the enameled bricks, were new to history.

On the top of the ziggurat was the sanctuary of the god, the holy of holies. Inside the temple were other rooms for worship, and also a school where boys were taught reading and writing, arithmetic, algebra and geometry.

Babylonian Society

At the top of Babylonian society were the king and his officials, the army officers and priests, the rich merchants, manufacturers, and owners of large estates. Rich merchants and priests acted as bankers and granted credits and loans, which helped trade. Goods were exchanged by "barter" — by giving so much wheat, for example, for a cow. Babylonia had no coinage, but there was a standard of established weights of metals. The standard weight was called a "talent," and this was divided into sixty "minas"; each mina weighed a pound and contained sixty shekels. Though sixty was used as a unit, the decimal system was also known.

The second class of Babylonian society was made up of laborers and farmers. Many of the laborers were highly skilled craftsmen whose shops turned out finely woven and brilliantly colored linens and woolens; beautiful furniture; gold, silver, glass and bronze

THE BABYLONIAN EMPIRE

vases and other wares; magnificent objects of lapis lazuli. The chief industry was brickmaking.

Farmers lived much as they had in Sumerian days. They raised the same grain, fruit, and vegetables, and tended the same barnyard animals.

The bottom class of Babylonian society consisted of the slaves. These were people captured in war, or those who were too poor to pay their debts. The law protected them carefully. It is said that a slave could own property, and eventually buy his freedom. The law also protected the free laborers and regulated their wages and the prices of what they made.

26

The family was the chief unit of Babylonian society. A man had one wife. He might divorce her (divorce was difficult for a woman), but the general rule was to marry "for keeps." A marriage was performed before witnesses, as it is today, and the man gave the father of the bride a present known as "purchase money." The girl brought her own dowry — clothes, blankets, perhaps some property. The man was the head of the family, and had complete control over his children.

Of Gods and Planets

The Babylonians believed that when people died they went to the lower world and lived unhappily in a huge cave. The prospect was gloomy enough to make them want as pleasant a life as possible here on earth. They believed that one of the ways to make sure of a happy life was to pay proper respect to the gods by worshiping them. Their chief gods were Marduk, greatest of all, and Ishtar, goddess of love and fertility.

Like the Sumerians, the Babylonians built towering temples to house their gods. Priests cared for the temples and conducted formal worship, in which the sacrifice of animals played an important part.

Concerned as they were with happiness in this world, the Babylonians were anxious to know what the gods had in store for them. The priests foretold the future in a number of ways, but the chief way was to examine the liver of an animal that was about to be sacrificed. A liver has a variety of markings — some common, others not. If certain markings predominated, the priest might say that the future looked good; if certain other signs predominated, he might say that the future was going to be a black one.

The Babylonians believed that the gods spoke to them and also

Dragon made of molded mud bricks.

revealed the future in the movements of the planets. The priests watched carefully the movements of the sun and the moon and the five planets they knew — Venus, Jupiter, Mars, Mercury, and Saturn.

The zodiac is an imaginary belt in the heavens which includes the paths of the sun, moon, and planets. The Babylonians divided this belt into twelve parts and gave each part a name and a sign. One part, for example, they called "Leo," and made the lion its sign. Another they called "Taurus," and gave it the sign of the bull. As the planets moved into and out of the various parts of the zodiac, men's fortunes changed for better or worse — or so the Babylonians believed.

This way of studying the heavenly bodies is not called astronomy, which is a pure science, but is known rather as "astrology." Nevertheless, scientific astronomy benefited by the observations of the ancient astrologers. For example, by observing the movement of the moon, the Babylonians were able to divide the year into twelve months of twenty-nine and thirty days each. Since this gave them a year only 354 days, they added an extra month occasionally. They divided the day, not into twenty-four hours as we do, but into twelve double hours, each 120 minutes long. To measure the hours, they invented water clocks and sundials.

28

Horse trainer sculptured in stone.

Literature

Babylonian priests wrote books explaining how to drive away evil spirits, but the greater part of Babylonian literature consisted of long poems concerning real or imaginary heroes. Such poems are known as "epics." One Babylonian epic tells the story of Gilgamesh, who journeyed far and wide in search of immortal life. If this is a world of justice, Gilgamesh asks, how does it happen that we have to die, even though we have done no wrong? The poem does not answer this familiar question.

Another epic describes the creation of the world by a single god, the coming of a great flood, and the building of a ship in which a single human family is saved. This poem was written about the time Abraham and his companions left Mesopotamia for Palestine. Once again we cannot help wondering whether they took some of these stories with them, since they resemble some of those in the Bible.

Sculpture

Strangely enough, in a land where people built towering palaces and temples, the finest art of the Babylonians was in miniature. Occasionally, stone statues were placed in temples and palaces, but the sculptors generally turned out squat and unlifelike figures.

29

Babylonian cylinder and clay tablet bearing its impression.

This was because Mesopotamia had so little stone that sculptors were unable to practice enough to acquire real skill.

On the other hand, Babylonian artists learned to carve with exquisite beauty small cylinders of semiprecious stone. Each cylinder was decorated with the owner's name and the figure of a god. These beautiful little cylinders were used as seals. A man would roll his cylinder on the soft clay of an important document in the same way a man picks up his pen to sign a letter today. Thousands of these cylinders have been found by archeologists, for the Babylonians liked to sign everything they could — letters, business agreements, wills, and so on.

Hammurabi (1800 B.C.)

The man who brought Babylonia to this high peak of civilization was a king named Hammurabi. He ruled with absolute power — though he had officials to help him — for more than forty years, beginning about 1800 B.C. With his well-trained army Hammurabi created an empire that stretched as far west as Syria on the Mediterranean coast. His soldiers were drawn from the ranks of ordinary citizens, while their officers came from the rich and the noble. Hammurabi supplied his army with food and clothes, but both officers and soldiers furnished their own bows and arrows, bronze spears, axes, swords, and shields.

The greatest achievement of the Babylonians was to take the old Sumerian laws and develop them into the most elaborate and fairest collection of laws that the world had yet seen or was to see for centuries. It was done at Hammurabi's direction, and so is known as "Hammurabi's Code."

The laws were written on a slab of black diorite (a granular stone) about eight feet high. Today it is in the famous Louvre Museum in Paris. At the top of the stone is carved Hammurabi standing before Shamash, the sun god. Shamash, with sun rays behind his shoulders, is seated on his throne and is handing the great Code of Laws to Hammurabi. The rest of the stone is covered

Hammurabi with some of his laws.

A Babylonian "kudukka," a carving on stone.

with 3,600 lines of writing, which give all the laws included in Hammurabi's Code. These laws cover both civil and criminal matters and regulate almost everything in life. For example, they specify the price of labor and animals. They apply to property and trade, contracts and wills, business and agriculture. They protect the rights of women, children, and slaves, and also designate penalties for hurting a person or his property. The basis of Babylonian criminal law was what we call "retaliation" — that is to say, "an eye for an eye, and a tooth for a tooth."

The courts administering the law were located either in temples or government buildings. Cases were tried in the towns where they originated, but if a man wanted to appeal to the king, he could.

Nebuchadrezzar II

The Babylonians were wise to adopt so much of the wonderful Sumerian civilization. But then, unfortunately for them, they grew satisfied with the past and stopped inventing and thinking for themselves. After Hammurabi's death, the Babylonians produced few ideas of importance. And then, for a time, they were conquered by the Assyrians from the rolling hill country of the upper Tigris.

Then, in the sixth century B.C., a new and invigorating spirit arose in Babylon. A Semitic people known as the Chaldeans drove out the Assyrians and moved into the country. The Chaldeans had only one king of any importance, but he was an extraordinary man. His name was Nebuchadrezzar II, and he ruled from 604–562 B.C.

During his long reign at Babylon, Nebuchadrezzar extended the frontiers of his Chaldean Empire from the Persian Gulf to Asia Minor and Egypt. In 586 B.C. he captured Jerusalem, destroyed its temple, and brought the Hebrews back to Babylon. Here they stayed in captivity for fifty years, until a Persian king let them return to Jerusalem.

Nebuchadrezzar had a beautiful wife who was homesick for the mountains of Media to the east, where she had grown up. So that she might have something tall to look at in the flat Babylonian countryside, Nebuchadrezzar built a huge ziggurat and planted trees and bushes on its terraces. These became known as the "Hanging Gardens of Babylon," and were regarded as one of the Seven Wonders of the ancient world.

On top of the ziggurat, Nebuchadrezzar built a temple for the worship of Marduk. The ziggurat and temple together rose three hundred feet above the earthen mound on which the building stood. One side of the ziggurat measured 1,360 feet at its base.

The Hebrews, who were in Babylon at this time, probably brought home stories of this tall tower when they were allowed to return to Jerusalem. In the Bible, they called it the "Tower of Babel," the foundation stone of heaven and earth, resting on the underworld and reaching to the sky.

During his reign, Nebuchadrezzar strongly fortified Babylon. Around the city he built a wall twelve miles in circumference, and twenty-five feet thick. This wall was made of brick and bitumen (a kind of asphalt), and its top was broad and smooth enough to accommodate a four-horse chariot. All along the top were towers from which the king's soldiers could watch the surrounding plain and cast their weapons at attackers.

The most famous gate in the wall was the Gate of Ishtar. Like the wall, it was made of baked bricks, and it was faced with magnificent enameled tiles in blue, red, yellow, and white. These tiles pictured lions and other animals, and also monsters such as dragons. From this Gate of Ishtar, named for the great Semitic Mother Goddess, religious processions moved down a broad "festival avenue" to the temple of Marduk, Babylon's chief god. Marduk's temple was made of baked brick and, like the gate, was faced with colorful enamel tiles picturing real and fanciful animals. It was 280 feet long and 265 feet wide. The shrine of the god was in an inside court measuring 125 by 100 feet.

Nebuchadrezzar's palace was built in the same style as the temple. Its entrance was guarded by huge lions carved in basalt (a black rock). Inside, the floor was of sandstone. Some of the sculptures on the walls were made of a blue paste. The palace contained a large number of official and private rooms, and also four courtyards.

Babylon clearly reached great heights in the days of Hammurabi (1800 B.C.) and Nebuchadrezzar (600 B.C.). During the centuries between the reigns of these two kings, Babylon was conquered by the Assyrians. To the southwest, Egypt flourished for a time, and so did the land of the Hittites in Asia Minor. There were also two tiny states of note: Phoenicia, along the Syrian coast, and Palestine. It was the Phoenicians who invented the alphabet we now use, and who spread it across the seas on their famous trading voyages. It was the Hebrews in Palestine who created one of the world's great religions. Meanwhile, a politically important state, one destined to build a powerful empire, was growing in strength. This was Assyria, situated amid the cool hills of northern Mesopotamia, along the upper Tigris.

The Gate of Ishtar.

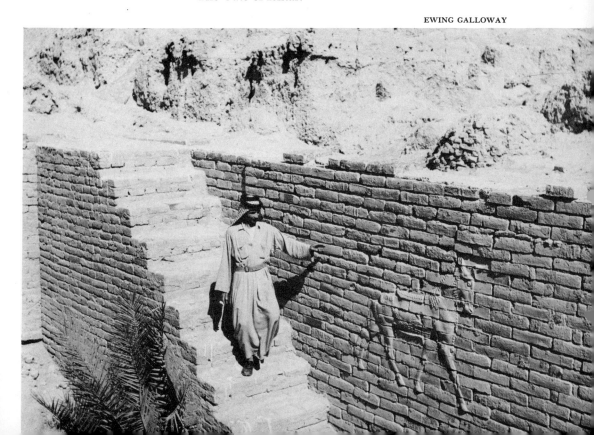

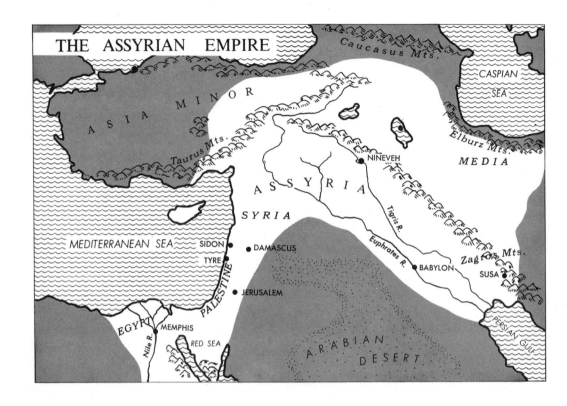

The Assyrians

THE ASSYRIANS were a vigorous Semitic people who formed a compact nation. Their civilization was based on that of Sumer and Babylonia. Because they relied on the past, they did little original thinking of their own, but they were very successful in taking what other people had learned and arranging it in useful fashion. For example, their most famous king, Ashurbanipal, founded two huge libraries at his capital, Nineveh. The contents of these libraries consisted chiefly of thousands of copies of Babylonian writings on cuneiform clay tablets. It was the Assyrians, however, with their powerful armies who saved Mesopotamian civilization from being destroyed by wild nomads from the north.

The truth is that the chief activity of the Assyrians was war, and they were fortunate in having a line of able kings to wage it. It was Sargon II (722–705 B.C.) who brought Palestine under Assyrian rule. Then his son, Sennacherib (705–681 B.C.) conquered Egypt. The great Ashurbanipal (669–626 B.C.) ruled over a territory that included Babylonia and stretched from Media (east of the Persian Gulf) to Asia Minor, and took in Syria, Palestine, and Egypt. Never before had the world seen so large an empire.

Carving in alabaster of King Ashurbanipal hunting.

The Assyrian Empire

The special importance of the Assyrian Empire lies in its fair system of governing the areas, or provinces, that it conquered. The system was copied by the Persians, who came after them, by Alexander the Great, and finally by the Romans.

Each Assyrian province had a governor who was appointed by the king and was strictly controlled by him. The duty of the governor was to protect his province with troops, collect taxes, and administer justice. All the provinces, even those far from the capital, were ruled in the same way.

When a province revolted, it was cruelly punished. History shows us that all people have been cruel occasionally, but for the Assyrians, terror, torture, and destruction were almost a way of life. They skinned their enemies alive, butchered them, and stuck their bodies up on poles. To keep the people in conquered countries from rebelling, the Assyrians often transplanted them from one part of their empire to another. In fairness we must add that we would not know so much about Assyrian cruelty if they themselves had not boasted of it in their written records.

The Army

Obviously, to judge by its successes, the Assyrian army was very effective as a fighting force. Many Assyrians made it their career. Officers, drawn from the nobility, commanded troops made up of artisans and farmers. These men were disciplined and well drilled. There were cavalry troops, warriors in horse-drawn battle chariots, and also heavily armed infantry with shields and fine iron spears and swords. The light-armed troops consisted of archers, famous for the accuracy of their shots, and slingers who could hurl fairly heavy stones a considerable distance.

38

Prisoners of war being led into exile.

The Assyrian army also included men who were trained to dig under the walls of an enemy's city and weaken them. Once this was done, the Assyrians would move up battering rams to knock down the walls. Their siege machinery included several platforms, raised one above the other and mounted on wheels, which could be rolled up against the enemy's walls so that the attackers could be on the same level as the defenders.

The Assyrians launched their attacks from camps that had been carefully fortified in advance. If the battle was in the open and not before a town, they fought in small, easily maneuvered units. Tac-

A winged Assyrian from the past looks down on a resident of modern Baghdad.

tically, these small units represented a new idea in warfare. They were far superior to the clumsy masses of men that other states used.

In order to keep their empire together, the Assyrians found that they must be able to move their armies quickly from one region to another. For this purpose they built many excellent roads. But the roads helped business and trade, too. Great caravans, protected by military posts here and there, moved safely across the deserts. Despite their brutality, the Assyrians brought peace to a large world, and this meant great unity and increased trade and prosperity for people in general.

Religion and Art

Although the Assyrians took many things from the Babylonians, they did not adopt the Babylonian god Marduk. The chief god of the Assyrians was Ashur, a fierce and warlike deity. Except for Ashur, the gods of the Assyrians and the Babylonians were much the same.

The Assyrians were a superstitious people. In order to overcome

A king and his cupbearer.

Human-headed bull guarding an
Assyrian palace.

their fear of men and evil spirits, they frequently sought the advice of priests. The priests spent a good deal of time watching solar and lunar eclipses in the belief that the gods might be sending messages. As in Babylon, interest in the heavens had more to do with astrology than astronomy.

The Assyrian artists, like those of Babylonia, cut beautiful seals. Unlike the Babylonians, they had a plentiful supply of stone from the hills round about. They built their palaces and temples with stone, although they often used baked bricks for walls.

42

Sculptured figures on a temple wall.

In front of their palaces and temples, the Assyrians frequently put tremendous human-headed bulls, carved from stone, to serve as guardians and protectors of the buildings. On the inside walls they carved pictures of Assyrians, and especially of their kings, fighting and hunting. The human figures are so bundled up in heavy clothes that they cannot compare in beauty and realism with the animal carvings. The Assyrians have never been surpassed in their carvings of wounded animals, in which both strength and pain are marvelously portrayed.

43

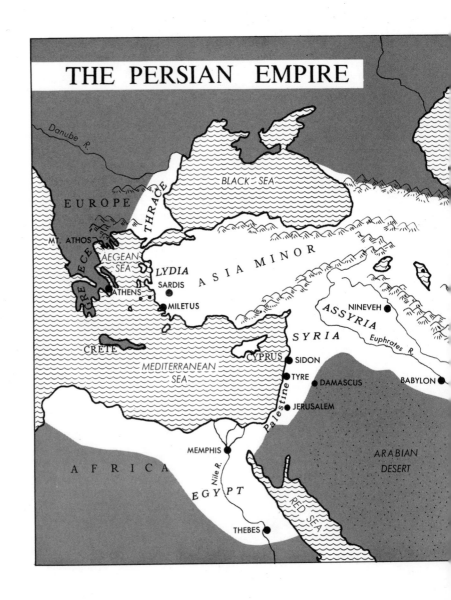

THE PERSIAN EMPIRE

Danube R.

BLACK SEA

EUROPE

THRACE

MT. ATHOS

AEGEAN SEA

GREECE

ATHENS

LYDIA

SARDIS

MILETUS

ASIA MINOR

ASSYRIA

NINEVEH

SYRIA

Euphrates R.

CRETE

CYPRUS

SIDON

TYRE

DAMASCUS

BABYLON

MEDITERRANEAN SEA

Palestine

JERUSALEM

MEMPHIS

AFRICA

Nile R.

ARABIAN DESERT

EGYPT

RED SEA

THEBES

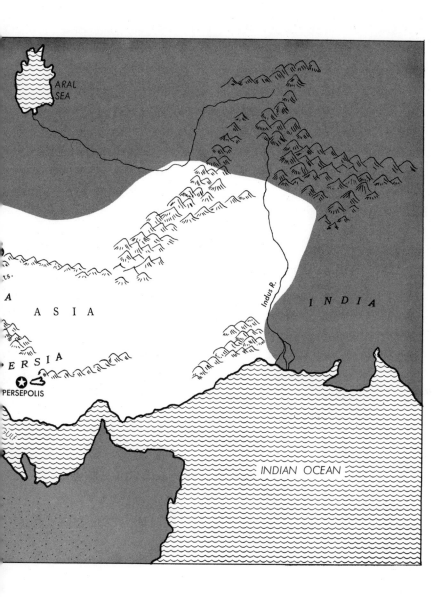

ARAL
SEA

ts.

A

A S I A

ERSIA

Indus R.

I N D I A

★
PERSEPOLIS

GULF

INDIAN OCEAN

The Mighty Persian Empire

IN 612 B.C., Scythians, Medes, Persians, and other enemies of the Assyrians combined to destroy Nineveh, capital of Assyria. Then, in 539 B.C., after the death of the great king, Nebuchadrezzar, the Persians captured Babylon. Semitic power in the Near East came to an end, and the Persian Empire began its rise.

Persia lies east of Mesopotamia and today is generally called Iran. Its modern capital is at Tehran, about sixty-five miles south of the Caspian Sea, near the towering Elburz Mountains, but in ancient times its capital was far to the south, at Persepolis.

It was Cyrus the Great (550–529 B.C.) who started the Persians on their famous career in history. Not only did he conquer the neighboring Medes and the Babylonians, but he also marched into Asia Minor. Here he overthrew Croesus, the fabulously wealthy king of Lydia. He then turned to the Greek cities along the coast facing the Aegean Sea and conquered them. To the east, he pushed the frontiers of the Persian Empire as far as India. His son, Cambyses, conquered Egypt.

The Persians belonged to the same Indo-European branch of the human race as did the Greeks and Romans. Within their mighty empire that stretched from Europe to India, taking in the entire ancient Near East, there were many different races. These races lived at peace with one another. There were no tariff barriers; instead, there was unified trade. The Persian Empire serves to remind us that men have found it possible to unite a very large part of the civilized world in one state.

One reason for the Persian Empire's success was the Persians' tolerance of the religions and customs of the people they conquered. Cyrus the Great set the pattern by letting the Hebrews

46

Cliff tombs near Persepolis. Darius the Great is believed to be buried here.

(who had been brought to Babylon by Nebuchadrezzar) end their captivity and return to Palestine.

Darius I

The real organizer of the Persian Empire was Darius I, who was one of the great administrative geniuses of history. His reign followed that of Cambyses, and lasted from 522 to 486 B.C. It was he who carved the inscription on the rock at Behistun that was so

47

helpful to scholars trying to decipher the cuneiform writing of the Sumerians.

This great Persian organizer and administrator was an absolute monarch who ruled by the grace of God. He had the high-sounding title of "The Great King, King of Kings." People who came into his presence had to prostrate themselves — lie flat, with their faces to the ground. A council of Persian nobles, however, held his immense power in check.

Darius adopted the Assyrian plan of dividing the empire into provinces, or satrapies, as they were called. The satraps, or governors of the provinces, were completely under the control of the king. Their job was to protect their satrapies, collect taxes, and administer justice. A powerful official representing the king and known as "the King's Eye" was constantly on the move throughout the empire. His duty was to report to the king whether the satrapies were well governed and prosperous.

Much of the work of governing the Persian Empire was carried on in Susa, a city to the northwest of Persepolis. A special road, known as the "Royal Road," ran for a distance of 1,500 miles from Susa to Sardis, the former capital of the Lydian Empire in Asia Minor. But this was only one of the many fine roads the Persians built to connect the various parts of their empire, promote trade, and make it possible to move their armies in times of danger. Letters were carried along these roads by mounted messengers who found fresh horses waiting for them at regular intervals.

Throughout the whole Persian Empire there were uniform weights, measures, and coinage. The gold coin was known as a "daric" (named after Darius) and was worth about $6.00. There were silver and bronze coins, too. The peace that Persia brought to Asia produced a wonderful prosperity.

48

Rock carvings depicting the conquests of Darius the Great.

The Attack on Greece

The Greeks in the conquered coastal cities of Asia Minor were very valuable to Darius as sailors and traders. They and the Phoenicians formed the Persian navy. It was not long before Darius began to think how greatly he would strengthen his empire if he conquered Greece proper — the European peninsula across the Aegean Sea from Asia Minor. If he had succeeded, free Greek civilization would have stopped developing and our civilization today, which is based on the Greek, would be different.

In 492 B.C. Darius sent a huge army and navy across the Hellespont. But the fleet was wrecked off the nearby promontory of Mount Athos, and the army had to return to Asia. Without the fleet,

Ruins of a Persian palace.

THREE LIONS

Drinking cup made of gold.

the soldiers would not have had enough food to eat. Two years later, Darius sent a second and smaller fleet across the Aegean Sea to attack Athens. On the nearby plain of Marathon, the citizens of Athens won a victory that has been famous ever since.

Then Darius I died, and the new king, Xerxes, spent the next years carefully planning still another invasion of Greece. One of the things he did was to dig a canal through the promontory of Mount Athos, so the navy would not have to sail around it.

In 480 B.C. Xerxes struck. His army won a victory at the Pass of Thermopylae, but his navy was utterly defeated in the Bay of Salamis, off Athens. Greece was saved, and the Greek cities along the coast of Asia Minor were liberated.

The rest of the mighty Persian Empire stood until late in the next century, when Alexander the Great came out of Greece to overthrow it (330 B.C.). For the remainder of antiquity, the chief lands that Persia had ruled belonged first to the successors of Alexander, and then to Rome.

51

Silver antelope, designed to be worn as a pendant.

Persian Art and Religion

Herodotus, the great Greek historian of ancient times, tells us that the Persians educated their children "in three things only — in riding, in shooting, and in speaking the truth." Probably this was true of the Persians early in their history, while they had a very simple life in the mountains. But if we look at the ruins of their magnificent palace at Persepolis, which Alexander the Great burned in 330 B.C., we can be sure that they became as luxurious and skillful in the arts as other people of antiquity.

The Persians borrowed from the Babylonians the idea of erecting the palace on a huge platform. But they built the whole building of stone, rather than brick, since there was a plentiful supply of stone in their country.

Large stairways rose from ground level to the terrace of the palace. These were really ceremonial stairways — used for royal ceremonies and processions. The sculptures that decorated them depicted a New Year's festival. Some show foreign ambassadors bringing to the king tribute such as horses, clothes, and bracelets. Still others show religious scenes, and the king fighting with lions. At the top of the stairways, the terrace leads to the royal hall, full of tall and graceful columns. Here the Persian kings welcomed foreign dignitaries and entertained at impressive receptions and banquets. Other parts of the palace were given over to the private

The royal palace at Persepolis.

dwelling rooms of the king and his family. The entire inside of the building was decorated with beautiful colored tiles.

As the Persian Empire grew stronger and more prosperous, the religious beliefs of the people matured and changed. In the beginning, the Persians worshiped many gods, especially those that represented the powers of nature. The priests were a special group called Magi, who thought they could win the favor of the gods and drive out evil spirits by the use of magic charms. The English word "magic" comes from the name for these priests.

Then, during the sixth century B.C., a great religious leader was born in Persia. His name was Zoroaster. As Zoroaster grew up, he was greatly puzzled by the fact that both good and evil existed in the world. Why, he asked himself, did not the all-powerful gods cast out evil and make the whole world good? It was a problem that had disturbed men before him, but Zoroaster believed he had found the answer. There was one supreme god who had created heaven and earth and man. He was the god of light, Ahura Mazda, and he was forever at war with the powers of darkness, or evil. Zoroaster taught that those who supported Ahura Mazda would win eternal life, but those who conspired with the powers of darkness would fall into a pit full of demons. The Persians worshiped Ahura Mazda on hilltops, with blazing fires. Drink offerings and prayers formed part of the ceremony.

The Legacy of the Ancient Near East

By TRADE and conquest the Babylonians spread much of their civilization — which came from the Sumerians — over the ancient world. The Syrians of the eastern Mediterranean coast took many ideas from the Babylonians, including their art and their way of

The great ceremonial gate at Persepolis.

A room in the palace at Persepolis.

constructing arches. Then the Syrians and the Phoenician traders carried this mixed civilization further west, to the Greeks and Etruscans and Romans in Europe.

The Hebrews adopted some religious ideas from the Babylonians. The Greeks borrowed the Babylonian system of weights, their calendar, and a good deal of their science, especially their knowledge of the heavenly bodies. All ancient civilization was deeply in the debt of the Babylonians.

The genius of the Assyrians, on the other hand, was in admin-

56

istering the various parts of a large empire with equal skill and fairness. The Assyrian methods of administration were taken over and made even better by the Persians, who were especially tolerant of the religions and customs of other people. The Persians passed on a model form of imperial government to the Romans, the greatest empire builders of antiquity.

There is no mystery at all concerning the origin of our own western, European civilization. It is a mixture of the Hebrew–Christian religion, Greek literature and thought, Roman government and law.

As we develop our own fine civilization, we can learn two great lessons from the Babylonians. One is that peace and prosperity, good government, and beauty in life are likely to come about when people welcome vigorous new ideas and are willing to experiment. The second lesson is that when people copy the past too much and become very conservative, they are apt to stagnate and fall.

Index

FIRST BOOKS
Complete Check List

Series No.	Quantity	Title	Author	Listings	Grade Reading Level
68		Atlas	C S Hammond & Co	A sl L	3-4
22		Africa	Hughes	A sl L CS	4-7
140		Air	Knight	A sl L	4 up
1		Airplanes	Bendick	A sl L C CS	3-6
76		American History	Commager	A sl L C CS	4 up
11		The American Revolution	Morris	A sl L C CS	5 up
158		Ancient Bible Lands	Robinson	New Publication	
134		Ancient Egypt	Robinson	A L	4 up
110		Ancient Greece	Robinson	A L	4 up
150		Ancient Mesopotamia and Persia	Robinson	A L	4 up
99		Ancient Rome	Robinson	A L	4 up
73		The Antarctic	Icenhower	A L C	4-7
77		Archaeology	Kubie	A sl L C CS	4 up
135		Architecture	Moore	A sl L	4 up
104		Astronomy	Grey	A L	4 up
107		Australia	Kaula	L	4 up
5		Automobiles	Bendick	A sl L C CS	3-5
44		The Ballet	Streatfeild	A sl L CS	4-7
148		Barbarian Invaders	Sobol	A	5 up
14		Baseball	Brewster	A sl L C CS	3-5
94		Basketball	Schiffer	A sl L C	4-8
4		Bees	Tibbets	A L C CS	3-6
98		Bells	Fletcher	L CS	2-4
18		Birds	Williamson	A sl L C CS	3-6
2		Boats	Gossett	A L CS	2-4
101		Boys' Cooking	Beim	A sl L C CS	4 up
149		Brazil	Sheppard	A	4 up
43		Bridges	Peet	A L C CS	3-7
6		Bugs	Williamson	A sl L C CS H	3-5
153		California Gold Rush	Havighurst	A L	4-7
65		Canada	C & M Lineaweaver	A L C	4-6
139		Cartoons for Kids	Fenner		2-5
111		Cats	Taber	A sl L C	3-6
54		Caves	E Hamilton	A sl L C	4-6
45		Chess	Leeming	A sl L C CS H	5 up
173		The China Clippers	Rich	New Publication	
146		Christmas Joy	Wilson	A L	1-3
105		Civil War Land Battles	Dupuy	A sl L C	5 up
137		Civil War Naval Actions	Dupuy	A sl L	5 up
29		Codes and Ciphers	S & B Epstein	A sl L C CS H	3-5
95		Color	Paschel	A L C CS	5 up
157		Comunist China	Kinmond	New Publication	
108		The Congo	McDonnell	L	3-6
9		Congress	Coy	A sl L C H	5 up
47		Conservation	F C Smith	A sl L C CS	4-7
85		The Constitution	Morris	A sl L C	5 up
40		Cotton	Rogers	A L C CS	4-6
13		Cowboys	Brewster	A sl L C	4 up
10		Dogs	Taber	A L C CS	3-5
39		Dolls	H Hoke	A sl L C CS	1-3
88		Drawing	Slobodkin	A sl L C	6 up
96		The Early Settlers	Rich	A sl L C	4-6
81		The Earth	Sevrey	A L C	5 up
42		Electricity	S & B Epstein	A sl L C CS	4-8
83		England	Streatfeild	A L C CS	4-7
26		Eskimos	Brewster	A sl L C CS	3-5
79		Fairy Tales	Abell		3 up
25		Festivals	Reck	A L C	3-6
21		Firemen	Brewster	A L	3-5
69		Food	Scheib	A L C CS	3-5
87		Football	Schiffer	A sl L C	3 up
92		France	Gottlieb	A sl L C	4-7
61		Gardening	Kirkus	A sl L C	4-6
122		Ghana	Lobsenz	A sl L	4-7
155		Glaciers	Marcus	A L	4 up
60		Glass	S & B Epstein	A L C CS	3-5
48		Hawaii	S & B Epstein	A L C CS	4-6
62		Holidays	Burnett	A L	3-5
8		Horses	McMeekin	A sl L C CS	5 up
129		How to Fix It	Bendick-Berk	A sl L	3 up
143		Human Senses	Liberty	A sl L	4 up
66		India	Hahn	L C CS	4-7
103		The Indian Wars	Morris	A	4 up
15		Indians (American)	Brewster	A L C CS	2-6
41		Israel	Kubie	A sl L C CS	4-7
89		Italy	S & B Epstein	A sl L C CS	4-7
30		Japan	Mears	A L C CS	4-7
58		Jazz	Hughes	A L C CS H	7 up
19		Jokes	Chrystie	A L C CS	3-6
130		Kings	Newton	L	3-6
172		Language & How To Use It	Applegate	New Publication	
159		Legendary Beings	Jacobson	New Publication	
74		Letter Writing	Jacobson	A L C CS	4-6
160		Light	Harrison	New Publication	
152		Machines	Buehr	A	3-6
46		Magic	Stoddard	A sl L C CS	3-5
75		Mammals	Williamson	A sl L C CS H	4 up
90		Maps and Globes	S & B Epstein	A sl L C CS	4-6
125		Measurement	S & B Epstein	L	4-6
102		Medieval Man	Sobol	A sl	4 up
123		The Mediterranean	Gottlieb	A L	4-7
63		Mexico	S & B Epstein	A L C H	4-7
35		Microbes	Lewis	A sl L C CS H	4 up
116		Mining	Markun	A L	3-6
51		Music	Norman	A sl L C	3-6
128		Mythical Beasts	Jacobson	A L	3-5
67		Mythology	Elgin	A sl L CS	4 up
113		National Monuments	Lobsenz	A L	3 up
115		National Parks	Lobsenz	A L	3 up
27		Negroes	Hughes	A sl L C CS	4 up
154		Netherlands	Cohn	A	4 up
12		New England	Rich	A L CS H	4-6
119		New World Explorers	Rich	A L	4-6
131		New Zealand	Kaula	A	4 up
72		Norse Legends	Elgin	L	4-6
16		Nurses	Elting	A sl L C CS	3-5
133		Ocean	Epstein	A	4 up
109		The Oregon Trail	Havighurst	A L C	3-7
118		Paintings	Moore	A sl L C	4 up
151		Pakistan	Bothwell	A L	4 up
84		The Panama Canal	Markun	A sl L C	4 up
50		Photography	J Hoke	A sl L C CS H	5 up
142		Physical Fitness	Walsh	A L	4 up
97		Pioneers	Havighurst		4-8
38		Plants	Dickinson	C CS	4 up
37		Poetry	Peterson	A sl L C CS	3-6
53		Prehistoric Animals	Dickinson	A sl L C CS	4-7
28		Presidents	Coy	A L CS	4-6
64		Printing	S & B Epstein	A sl L C CS H	5 up
114		Public Libraries	Graham	L	2-4
24		Puppets	Jagendorf	A L C	3-5
49		Rhythms	Hughes	A sl L C CS	2-4
55		Roads	Bothwell	A sl L C CS	3-5
136		Sailing	M Lineaweaver	A L C CS	8 up
31		Science Experiments	Wyler	A sl L C	4-6

ALL are supplied in the Watts Guaranteed Library Binding

ALL are in large, clear type

ALL are fully illustrated—many with over 100 pictures, and in color

ALL checked and double-checked for accuracy, authority, and clarity of text

ALL 7¼ x 8¾ size

KEY TO LISTINGS:

A American Library Association, Booklist

sl Booklist, Small Library Listing

L Library Journal

C H. W. Wilson Company, Children's Catalog

CS Child Study Association of America, Books of the Year for Children

H H. W. Wilson Company, High School Catalog

Write for catalog. Address Dept. Sc

FRANKLIN WATTS, INC. A Division

575 Lexington Avenue   New York 22, N. Y.   of Grolier Incorporated

What they say about
FIRST BOOKS

"Their wide appeal, their broad coverage of varied subject areas, their wide range of significant and timely topics, and their attractive format and illustrations have made them valuable library materials."

MIRIAM PETERSON
Chicago Board of Education

"The format of each book has been superior and the books show that careful attention has been given to design, type, illustration, paper, and binding."

CAROLYN W. FIELD
Philadelphia Public Library

"I have long felt that the FIRST BOOKS developed (by Franklin Watts) were among the important creative contributions made by a publisher in recent decades."

PROF. HAROLD G. SHANE
Indiana University

"I really don't know how we ever ran our school libraries without the FIRST BOOKS!"

ELIZABETH HODGES
Baltimore Board of Education

"In covering a topic thoroughly, these books are like a junior encyclopedia, with an illustrated volume for each subject."

Christian Science Monitor

"Indeed an achievement! The high quality which has been maintained throughout the series is even more remarkable."

RUTH HILL VIGUERS
The Horn Book

"The FIRST BOOKS have made a real contribution in extending the horizons of their readers beyond the interests they knew they had."

JOSETTE FRANK
Child Study Association of America